### PRAISE FOR

'Zaina Ghani is one of poets. Her highly poet... and crafted, yet it leaves you breathless. This debut collection with The Emma Press, with all its freshness and originality, is one to savour.'
— Matthew M. C. Smith

'For Z.R. Ghani the colour red is the Borgesian aleph, the core, the sump, the source of everything: her own myths, narratives and traumas are cast in its supernal light. Her instrument is the finely honed and pellucid lyric, without the slightest hint of effort, overstatement or pretension. *In the Name of Red* is an exciting and highly sophisticated debut collection and Z.R Ghani is one to look out for.'
— Tim Liardet

POETRY PAMPHLETS
*Makeover*, by Laurie Bolger
*Accessioning*, by Charlotte Wetton
*Milk Snake*, by Toby Buckley
*Overlap*, by Valerie Bence

POETRY COLLECTIONS
*Europe, Love Me Back*, by Rakhshan Rizwan

SHORT STORIES AND ESSAY COLLECTIONS
*About Us*, by Reda Gaudiamo, translated from Indonesian by Ikhda Ayuning Maharsi Degoul and Phillipa Barker
*Parables, Fables, Nightmares*, by Malachi McIntosh
*Blood & Cord: Writers on Early Parenthood*, edited by Abi Curtis
*How Kyoto Breaks Your Heart*, by Florentyna Leow
*Night-time Stories*, edited by Yen-Yen Lu

ART SQUARES
*The Strange Egg*, by Kirstie Millar, illus. by Hannah Mumby
*The Fox's Wedding*, by Rebecca Hurst, illus. by Reena Makwana
*Pilgrim*, by Lisabelle Tay, illustrated by Reena Makwana
*One day at the Taiwan Land Bank Dinosaur Museum*, written and illustrated by Elīna Eihmane

BOOKS FOR CHILDREN
*The Untameables*, by Clare Pollard, illus. by Reena Makwana
*Eggenwise*, by Andrea Davidson, illus. by Amy Louise Evans
*Balam and Lluvia's House*, by Julio Serrano Echeverría, tr. from Spanish by Lawrence Schimel, illus. by Yolanda Mosquera
*Na Willa and the House in the Alley*, by Reda Gaudiamo, translated from Indonesian by Ikhda Ayuning Maharsi Degoul and Kate Wakeling

# In the Name of Red
## ZR Ghani

with illustrations
by Louise Weir

THE EMMA PRESS

First published in the UK in 2024 by The Emma Press Ltd.
Poems © Z. R. Ghani 2024.
Cover design and interior artwork © Louise Weir 2024.

All rights reserved.

The right of Z. R. Ghani to be identified as the author of this work has been asserted in accordance with the Copyright, Designs and Patents Act 1988.

ISBN 978-1-915628-22-0

A CIP catalogue record of this book
is available from the British Library.

Edited by Sohini Basak.
Typeset by Emma Dai'an Wright.

Printed and bound in the UK
by the Holodeck, Birmingham.

The Emma Press
theemmapress.com
hello@theemmapress.com
Birmingham, UK

# CONTENTS

Reddest Red . . . . . . . . . . . . . . . . . . . . . . . . . . . . 1
The Art of Cloying . . . . . . . . . . . . . . . . . . . . . . . 3
Jupiter Fox . . . . . . . . . . . . . . . . . . . . . . . . . . . . . . 5
Pomegranate Seeds . . . . . . . . . . . . . . . . . . . . . . 6
Moths of the Red Room . . . . . . . . . . . . . . . . . . 7
Mother . . . . . . . . . . . . . . . . . . . . . . . . . . . . . . . . 8
Estella . . . . . . . . . . . . . . . . . . . . . . . . . . . . . . . . 9
Splitting the Moon . . . . . . . . . . . . . . . . . . . . . 10
Water Song . . . . . . . . . . . . . . . . . . . . . . . . . . . 11
The Great Golden Baby . . . . . . . . . . . . . . . . . 12
The Mad Ones . . . . . . . . . . . . . . . . . . . . . . . . 16
Earthkeeper . . . . . . . . . . . . . . . . . . . . . . . . . . 18
Taste of the River . . . . . . . . . . . . . . . . . . . . . . 19
Lycan Boy . . . . . . . . . . . . . . . . . . . . . . . . . . . . 20
Hades at the End of Summer . . . . . . . . . . . . . 22
The Red Queen . . . . . . . . . . . . . . . . . . . . . . . 23
The Gift . . . . . . . . . . . . . . . . . . . . . . . . . . . . . 24
Sunday Evening in the Heat Wave . . . . . . . . . 25
After the Trial . . . . . . . . . . . . . . . . . . . . . . . . . 26

*Afterword* . . . . . . . . . . . . . . . . . . . . . . . . . . . . . *28*
*Acknowledgements* . . . . . . . . . . . . . . . . . . . . . . *28*
*About the poet* . . . . . . . . . . . . . . . . . . . . . . . . . *29*

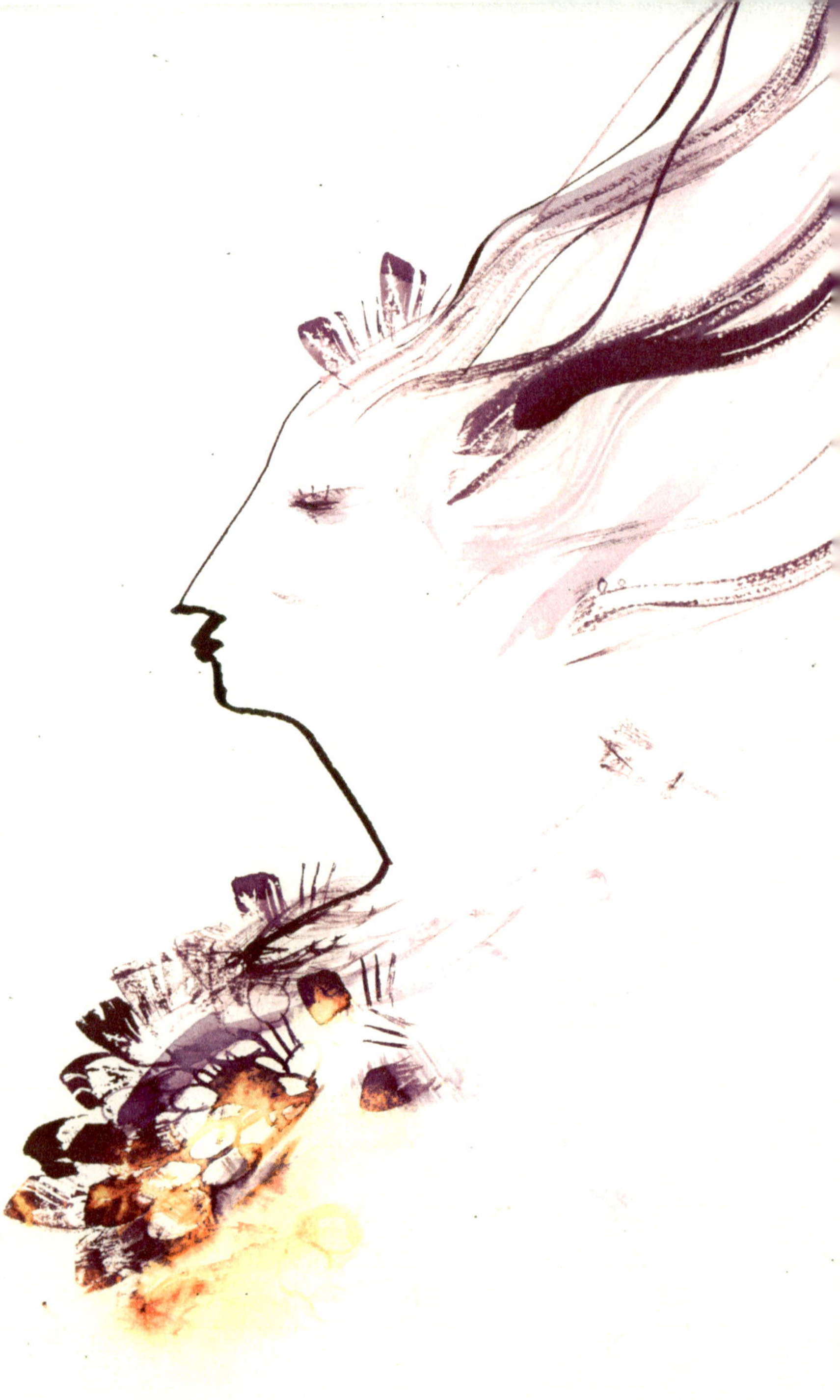

# *Reddest Red*

Be a darling and imagine. The reddest of all reds—
changeable in velvet, the usurper in broadcloth;
smooching the ground, cheek to cheek, in Louboutins.
I'm here, I'm always here, itching to breathe, vital
under your skin, trumpeted by pulse. I need to exist,
as the poison arrow's target; dirty on the warrior's face;
a flag rippling like a dragon overhead.
You wish you could know my names, all secret,
sacred, and true, but call me whatever you want,
I don't care, or summon me as rose, claret, vermilion,
ladies-blush, lust; evoke me from ruddy, madder,
brazilwood, orchil, cochineal, urucum—I need
to exist. For no other colour in two lengths of cloth
makes a gentleman and keeps him that way,
and there's nothing I can't improve with a scandal,
though I'm happiest reclining on a girl's pretty lips,
pitying potential left to rot, lesser reds that shall
but one day bloom into me if they dare. Know me
as a fiesta in everything I star in: I tickle a tree
and it's autumn, I tap someone and they blush,
I storm into a battlefield and it's a field of poppies,
all the time living my best life, as I always will,

me, Shakti, dancing like a graceful madwoman
in the flames of a star, roaring myself redder
(yes, it's possible), and charging back down to Earth
in the pope's fresh socks, diving into a dazzling
Diwali of fireflies as they, for a flare-and-sigh,
jaunt through my impermanent soul. But I need
to exist. Shed me, if you must, on your wedding night:
sari cloth, petticoat, silk blouse swaying with the bed,
or pin me as a bindi on your third eye like a sun,
so when they look at you they'll see me first, exalted.

How fortunate I am to be a colour, let alone
Red.

# *The Art of Cloying*

A book can be loved to death and not die.
Look at how this one refuses to close. Place the weight
of the world on it and it may stop demanding attention.

And if you choose to settle within it—this book
I once read, but isn't mine—with the same intimacy
as seeing the painless birth of sunrise for the first time,
you'll find the smudge of fingertips where a cryptic word
struck a chord and grew familiar. Pen lines preserve
inspirations not to be forgotten. That's telling of love:
what was spotless became a kneaded bed of the curious.

If the cover is missing, then it has shaken its burden;
it's dearer than gold. It's known the caress of eyes
and wants more. Suppose you, not knowing this,
were to tape it back and suffocate the perceived disgrace?
Isn't love tousled in the word *novel*?

My sisters used to wrap their books in decorative paper
recycled from bygone weddings. Inside were curated
words of warning, warding off eyes behind the filigree.
I tore in with my shoes on and drew morbid faces.
I loved every page as they did—but a little differently.

The first book I knew and ever kissed was a Quran.
I peered at the words, but could not seize them,
so I untied the embroidered cloth with my clean hands;
the dizzying calligraphy lay under my eyes—bold—
like the gates of *Jannah* prohibiting girls who don't listen…
My tongue wrestled to weave sense amid my shattered selves;
my instincts grappled with Estella, Miss Sharp, Miss Eyre,
when I'd rummage their pages with laughter, tears, prayer.

# *Jupiter Fox*

The coldest winter we knew—wind like blades:
never a dull moment between their embrace,
shredded bare parchment into a vertigo of seagulls.

I watched you fall asleep then stole out,
in search of fire to light the wood. My spirit fluent,
but dragging its lump of meat. It wasn't down to you
to deforest my mind: ideas must be pared back,
but I was conscious of you waiting; in your eyes
I'm gardening, snuffing glowing desire to plant ashes.

When I blow away the clouds like charcoal dust,
the universe isn't waiting for me anymore.

Once, under an apple-heavy branch, I found my flame.
A fox wearing the storms of Jupiter, eyes of volcanic glass,
wrapping the footpath around his paw, drew me closer to him.

Confiding in me, I heard him say,
*If happiness isn't a bittersweet reward,*
*it isn't happiness at all.*

## *Pomegranate Seeds*

Swallowed them whole—jewels that my body
would hoard, giving new meaning to the word
*chest*, for you to lift the axe and undress me,
rubies dripping down my legs; I want someone,

you, to want me as a means to an end, a road
less taken. While you're down there, untangle
the knot of besotted butterflies—they need
not love in excess. They will inherit the spring
I robbed them of, that was ripped from me

before I could scream about ruling two worlds
but owning neither. Hear me shudder an age
too late. Am I a cold rose stripped of thorns?
My petals shall flock too close to the sun.

And while in pursuit of more treasures, you
may be distracted by a goodbye note, a whorl
of hair, the ghost of my mother's jewellery box
ballerina, twisting the night, as your hand misses
the doorknob moon—just before you're dust.

## *Moths of the Red Room*

Passing round a flame, we whisper of moths,
trembling in our nightshirts whiter than ghosts.

If a moth touches your eye, you'll go blind
or worse—you'll see nothing but red forever.

The Red Room operates in darkness,
so if you dare, step lightly in case of wings,

graze the tapestry, and glean from the textures:
nature's instinct needs no instructing.

One fruit for each one of us in the family.
the moths are needles needless of thread,

always stitching my fallen fruit back onto the tree.
My sisters joked that mine was troubled,

and overdue for the moths' intense unpicking.
They locked me in the Red Room with my bad fruit.

A keyhole-shaped glow captured a moth—
wings lust-red; eyeless eyelids blinking senseless,

scarred with embroidery, pearls like crystal balls,
misting the future—then assaulted by tears.

## *Mother*

There are reasons to grieve today.
Mother runs a cold tap
over slabs of laundry,
cursing the day she was born.
That unwashed stench of hospital—
flesh, sweat, placenta
lolls over me like a suicide.
Her fourth daughter is a week old;
I'm not the youngest anymore.
I can't help but steal glances,
though I'll soon hear haunting
thuds as she beats herself,
or threatens to drink bleach.

# *Estella*

Just remind me that I'm desirable.
You may kiss my hand, if you wish to feel
something I can't. Don't ask if I've buried
my heart, darker than chimney sweeps. Body
sealed inside a riddle, slippery walls—
a stuffed crow with a bright stare betraying
the scores of lovers that have turned to stone.
I nibble on affection. *Old owl-eyes,*
thickly clad in corset, crinoline, dress,
night-black, unfurling myself in London,
hunting for fresh flesh. I am my mother's
jewel—a showpiece, though a touch could slice.
      A star that suckles on darkness, I land
      beneath your shadow, your heart in my hand.

## *Splitting the Moon*

I am worthy of your gaze, Father—
it's morning but you'd rather
read in the dark about the prophet,
peace be upon Him, splitting
the moon asunder with a finger,
because how else will you
secure your place in *Jannah*
(the seventh one nearest the throne)?

But you haven't said hello
in years; the embarrassment
has burrowed a home in us
as we've lived—*together*,
and I wonder why marriage
is my only way out, while
you wonder why God took away
your only son, humoured you
with daughters as your burdens
to bear. And there's so much
that demands logic and patience,
perhaps only from my side,
things you'll deem unimportant,
things that will upset God.

# *Water Song*

The morning is a voice between the endpapers
of two empty villages, telling its fables of yore.
It settles like a traveller who calls their home
wherever their hat falls when the wind blows.

Sunset on mango skin is the swollen dawn,
urged from the unstirred tea of the riverbed.
Fine hairs iridescent on petals crane for

a better view. Now noontide. Blossoms sweat
their fragrance onto a fountain that spends
them hastily, unwilling to disturb its own silver.

But listen—
the water's song is a parable:
*I was a body of sorts, trilling, dancing,*
*idling. Everything I touched multiplied,*
*until the paintbrush kingfisher disrupted me*
*and perplexed all that I toiled to manifest.*

# *The Great Golden Baby*

### I

At the cusp of death,
the gates of his afterlife
blew open for us.
Legends defined rivers
of liquid diamonds—

### II

Great golden baby,
preserved in a terracotta womb,
kicking the crust open.
We lifted our gaze
like blooms at the sun.

### III

He will come no more,
great golden sunlight,
poised birds at his feet,
bees huddled over his lips.

### IV

A dry interval
between the rainy seasons—
a lull after the flood.
They longed for your counsel:
*Gold baby, rise.*
A vast sea of candlelight.

### V

Then—
my shiver trembles the quill—
you whined awake
and in our hearts we rested,
adapting to the strangeness.

### VI

I took my first steps
into smoke and shadow,
never looking back.
You undid yourself to me
in cogs, arcane scrolls, and rust.

### VII

They placed a ruby
in your skull, turquoise for eyes,
poured birdsong between your lips,
tampered the scrolls in your bowels,
imprisoned in filigree—

### VIII

Meditating, you said,
*What we depend on to live
lacks authority.*
In no particular haste,
as if you knew your ending.

### IX

Weathered with age,
I boast of kings and princes,
brocade palaces, joyous
maidens, jewelled flutes,
basking in what you promised.

### X

Among wisteria,
petals fall on the temple:
a fuss in the breeze.
A white panther shreds to snow.
I'm drunk; I wait with patience.

### XI

The sun rises still
and shines on a house that floats;
the grass is like jade.
They paint their statues in gold
and worship them in your name.

# *The Mad Ones*

When I was young, before I learned
to use the poison arrow,
my father warned me of the mad ones in the glade,
and marked my photograph red with urucum
so no one could steal my soul.

The elders chanted about the mad ones
scything entire villages in one swoop.
Now I know the song.

It's never quiet in the forest
just as it's never quiet in the mind.

We hunt for nothing but the mad ones.
They leave behind consequences:
dry stumps and stinking cavities,
a spillage of frantic insects,
and fatten their trucks with our past,
the blissful dreams of our ancestors,
hacked to the bone, chattering in the smoke—

Above me a macaw skims a pool of sky,
where the trees brought shade,
and sends me a scarlet feather.

When the trees breathe, we breathe.
For each tree that is massacred, or burned,
my soul sheds a leaf. How many more
until I am swept away for the unfamiliar
to take my place, until I discover my own sacred,
emerald tales blinking their last in the fire?

## *Earthkeeper*

What is the meaning of this, O Earthkeeper?
A world under a cloche of petrichor,
knuckled in roots; the trees have sucked
in their cheeks, the lake has pursed
its lips to powdery ice. The silence—sealed,
the cold—guarded, and the night
will soon shut up shop, but the branches stay
fishing for jewels in your sky.

And I've written off civilisation,
read the nuances: a flattened raindrop,
a tear in the cloud, a punctured shell,
a wounded bark, a dent in the water...

Earthkeeper, you need not wander,
feverish like the sun, whirling like the Earth
in your cloak of dishevelling autumn, mind
a chrysalis, journeys raucous as rain. You find
another room in your endless pocket
to wield nature for your ease: bottled river,
sharpened feather, boxed fire, polished stone.
But can you seize the spirit of heartwood,
or de-clutter the shimmer from the lake?

Let some things elude you, O Earthkeeper.

## *Taste of the River*

I remember in my mouth the taste of the river.
The rocks in my pockets felt familiar.
They were souvenirs from my father,
                           the lonesome traveller,
who chewed the fish's eyes
and gave me its opalescent flesh.

I once dreamt of settling into that photograph,
where I'm forcing a smile next to a happy sibling,
that split-second indifference caught forever.

# *Lycan Boy*

Liquid skies cupped in mud,
I splash on starlight—drenched,
blending my story with yours.

They say you should run away,
as if the Devil is after you,
if you see a naked man in the woods.

Tonight, I run to you.

As children we raced up to the lone house,
threw conkers at the witch's window
and set off at the creak of the door.

Now the night's curse seduces you;
the cold is your blanket;
the forest prizes your howl
as its native tongue.

My clothes are on the floor;
the ground comes and goes.
You find me shivering
like a compass needle.
No one will approve.

But I'm glad that virtue exists
so when I stray from it
I can feel as good as this.

# *Hades at the End of Summer*

I think of her as one of Klimt's women,
thinner than a willow tree, performing ablutions by a river
shaped like an arm reaching out for an apple.
Heart of scintillating youth, it floods its red,
swelling the roots of the underworld.

She will shade over me
and find me dreaming of her.

A flurry of vows, so lips,
a sign of moonlight, so eyes,
an end to abstinence, so we kiss.

# *The Red Queen*

There, the moon: chasing time, on a new high,
the wool over its eyes, unhinged, wild—
deserves a beating from her. Not wolfsong,
not my pinafore, tented up to my chin
for all woodland creatures to gawp at, will sober it.
*Have the mirrors been whispering to you again?*

Perhaps a child or a hedgehog forced into a ball, flung
by a flamingo, but never a woman I won't be. Lady,
you must be joking. Certainly a girl-turned-unhalal-pig
by the Red Queen. I came out to parade my body.
*She's always hungry for your head.*

White rabbit, weary father of my conscience,
I see through your desperate lies; portals choking
under the snow. I'll turn the key on *her* this time.
My skirt is barricaded and my hat cuts throats.
*You're outgrowing my house.*

I was not spun from gold, but my mother's fallen hair;
it's not easy to unravel me, harder yet to keep me still.
Her arms under the snow know the scent of my neck;
father serves shards of a shoe with a note, *Eat Me*.
*I've known her to shake with fury until her face is no more.*

## *The Gift*

All girls must sup with God one day,
when He'll give us our pomegranate.

No plate, no cutlery,
we'll untie the linen,
break past the indignant crust of fate.

Mother, I think of your fruit,
those tiny cherubs where seeds,
droplets of blood, should've been.
They didn't choir for your milk,
nor grimace as they met light,
but moon-faced, stiff, swaddled
in the silence you left exposed.

# *Sunday Evening in the Heat Wave*

I find myself alone again,
hassling the bookshelf for a poem
I once read about a man
who sounds like rain.

The train station at a somnolent hour—but cool—
gives the girl an excuse to imprint the mud
for the last time along metallic vertebrae.
The city is a duct-taped hostage in the backseat
of a car dashing through the nauseating
choreography of a monsoon; moisture and dust
mask as petrichor and aura.

At last—
the cane under his arthritic guidance taps
the rust, that voice

                              the crash of an urn.

## *After the Trial*

Swaddled in red-sky arms,
colder than valley stone.
Starlight spearing to burn.
My hands are tied as I walk
the one-way dream to eternity
where starving ghosts shriek
with the rising threads of rain.
The shame tires me the most.
Tears too far to wipe away.

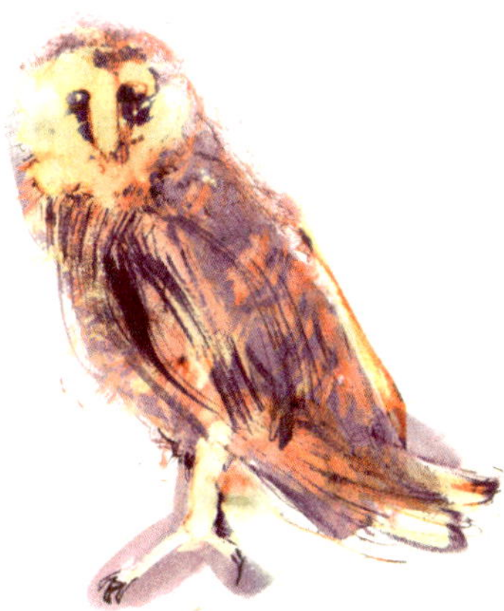

## AFTERWORD

Some of these poems feature characters from myths and novels: 'The Art of Cloying' mentions the characters Estella from *Great Expectations* by Charles Dickens, Rebecca Sharp from *Vanity Fair* by William Makepeace Thackeray, Jane Eyre from *Jane Eyre* by Charlotte Brontë. The poem 'Estella' is also inspired by the Charles Dickens character. The Red Room in 'Moths of the Red Room' is a symbol taken from *Jane Eyre*. The Greek deities Hades and Persephone and their story of love inspired 'Hades at the End of Summer', 'Pomegranate Seeds', and 'The Gift'. 'The Red Queen' mentions characters from Lewis Carroll's *Alice's Adventures in Wonderland*.

## ACKNOWLEDGEMENTS

First and foremost, I would like to thank Matthew M. C. Smith, poet and editor of *Black Bough Poetry*, who encouraged me to take my poetry writing seriously. Thank you for your generosity over the past few years. I couldn't have written these poems without you.

I would also like to thank the editor(s) of *Square Wheel Press, Magma, The Adriatic,* Sidekick Books, *The Storms Journal,* Nine Pens Press, *Fevers Of, The*

*Willowherb Review* and Arachne Press for publishing my poems/prose, a few of which appear in this collection. I'm immensely grateful to *Poetry Wales* for shortlisting a version of this pamphlet in their 2021 pamphlet competition.

I am so grateful to these exceptionally talented and generous poets for their boosts and support: Rhona Greene, Ankh Spice, Roger Hare, Andy MacGregor, and Regine Ebner.

Lastly, I owe my deepest gratitude to Sohini Basak and James Trevelyan at the Emma Press for believing in this collection. What an incredibly fulfilling journey it's been so far.

## ABOUT THE POET

Z. R. Ghani is from London. She graduated with a B.A. in Creative Writing from Bath Spa University in 2012. Her poems, which explore themes of identity, femininity, religion, and nature, have been published in literary journals such as *Magma, Black Bough Poetry, The Adriatic, The Willowherb Review, The Storms Journal,* and in various anthologies.

## ABOUT THE EMMA PRESS

The Emma Press is an independent publishing house based in the Jewellery Quarter, Birmingham, UK. It was founded in 2012 by Emma Dai'an Wright, and specialises in poetry, short-form prose and children's books.

The Emma Press has been shortlisted for the Michael Marks Award for Poetry Pamphlet Publishers in 2014, 2015, 2016, 2018, and 2020, winning in 2016.

In 2020-23 The Emma Press received funding from Arts Council England's Elevate programme, developed to enhance the diversity of the arts and cultural sector by strengthening the resilience of diverse-led organisations.

Website: theemmapress.com
Facebook, X and Instagram:
@TheEmmaPress